www.dixiechicks.com

A special thank you to Marion Kraft
for her assistance with this songbook.

Project Manager: CAROL CUELLAR
Book Art Layout: LISA GREENE MANE
Production Coordinator: DONNA SALZBURG
Album Art: © 2002 SONY MUSIC ENTERTAINMENT INC.
Photography: JAMES MINCHIN III
Album Art Direction: KEVIN REAGAN
Album Design: KEVIN REAGAN & BRET HEALEY
Stylist: AMY MINCHIN
Make-up: BILLY B., CANDY BURTON
Hair: TROY ZESTOS

600 MILES

HOME

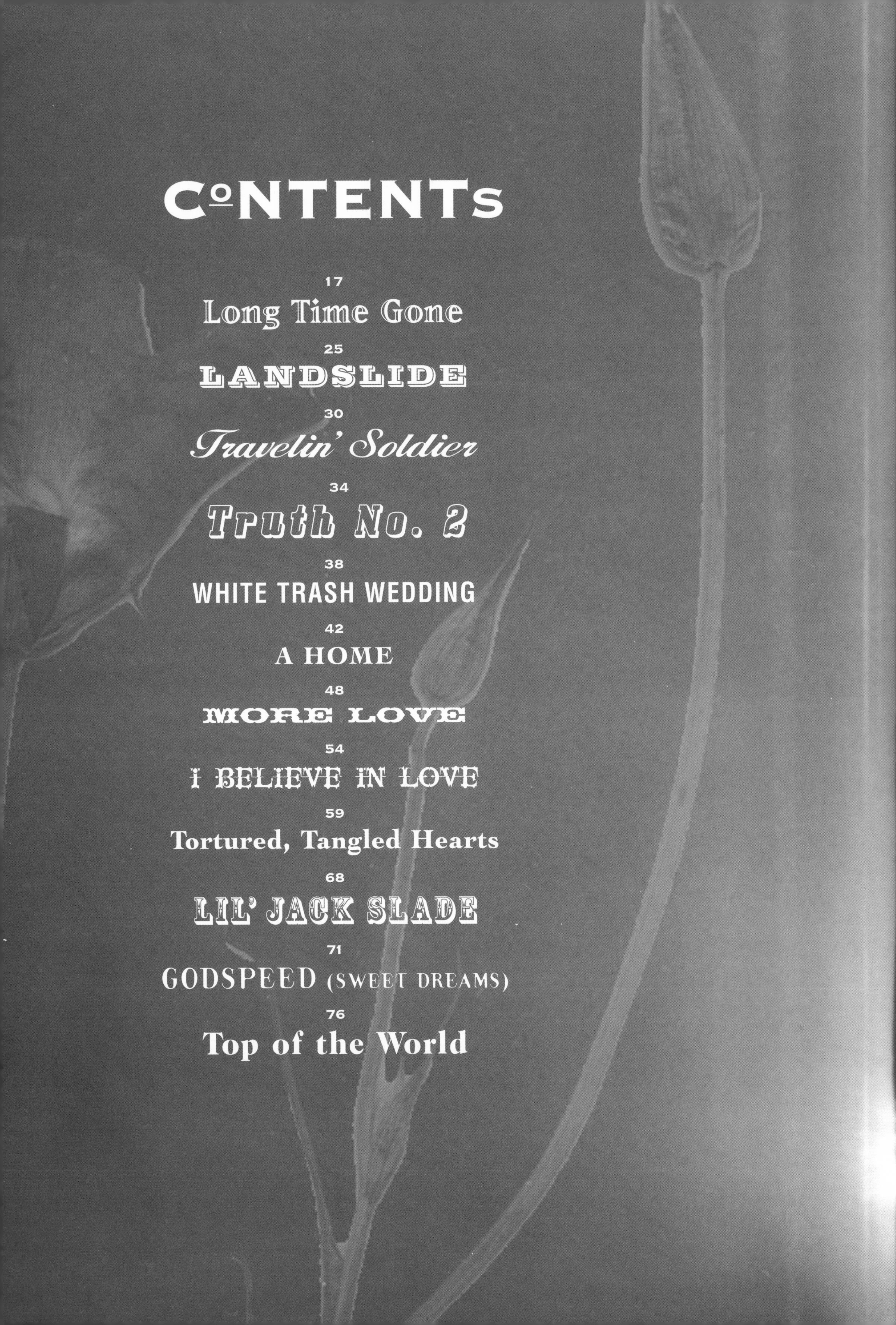

CoNTENTs

17
Long Time Gone

25
LANDSLIDE

30
Travelin' Soldier

34
Truth No. 2

38
WHITE TRASH WEDDING

42
A HOME

48
MORE LOVE

54
I BELIEVE IN LOVE

59
Tortured, Tangled Hearts

68
LIL' JACK SLADE

71
GODSPEED (SWEET DREAMS)

76
Top of the World

Cr.
BR
Quita
S.
Lockney
OF L
Floy
Dough
Petersbu
Co
Ral
Lorenzo
ck
CROS
South
GAR
Post
Justice
RDEN

Long Time Gone

WORDS & MUSIC BY DARRELL SCOTT

My daddy sits on the front porch swingin' / Lookin' out on a vacant field / Used to be filled with burly tobacco / Now he knows it never will / My brother found work in Indiana / Sister's a nurse at the old folks home / Momma's still cookin' too much for supper / And me I've been a longtime gone / Been a longtime gone / No I ain't hoed a row since I don't know when / Longtime gone / And it ain't comin' back again / Delia plays that ol' church piano / Sittin' out on her daddy's farm / She always thought that we'd be together / Lord I never meant to do her harm / Said she could hear me singin' in the choir / Me I heard another song / I caught wind and hit the road runnin' / And Lord I been a longtime gone / Been a longtime gone / Lord I ain't had a prayer since I don't know when / Longtime gone / And it ain't comin' back again / Now me I went to Nashville / Tryin' to be the big deal / Playin' down on Broadway / Gettin' there the hard way / Livin' from a tip jar / Sleepin' in my car / Hockin' my guitar / Yeah I'm gonna be a star / Now me and Delia singin' every Sunday / Watchin' the children and the garden grow / We listen to the radio to hear what's cookin' / But the music ain't got no soul / Now they sound tired but they don't sound haggard / They got money but they don't have cash / They got junior but they don't have hank / I think, I think, I think… the rest is… / A longtime gone / No I ain't hit the roof since I don't know when / Longtime gone / And it ain't comin' back I said / A longtime gone / No I ain't honked the horn since I don't know when / Longtime gone / And it ain't comin' back again / I said a longtime longtime longtime gone / Oh it's been a longtime / Longtime longtime longtime gone / Oh it's been a longtime gone / Longtime longtime longtime gone / Yeah yeah

LANDSLIDE

WORDS & MUSIC BY STEVIE NICKS

I took my love and I took it down / I climbed a mountain and I turned around / And I saw my reflection in the snow-covered hills / Well the landslide brought me down / Oh, mirror in the sky / What is love / Can the child within my heart rise above / Can I sail thru the changing ocean tides / Can I handle the seasons of my life / Well, I've been afraid of changing 'cause I built my life around you / But time makes you bolder / Children get older / I'm getting older too / Well…well, I've been afraid of changing 'cause I built my life around you / But time makes you bolder / Children get older / I'm getting older, too / Well I'm getting older too / So, take this love and take it down / Yeah and if you climb a mountain and ya turn around / And if you see my reflection in the snow-covered hills / Well the landslide brought me down / And if you see my reflection in the snow-covered hills / Well maybe / Well maybe / Well maybe the landslide will bring you down

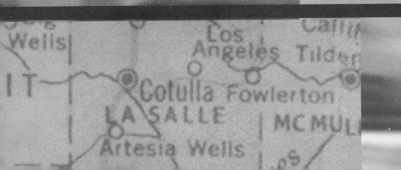

Travelin' Soldier

WORDS & MUSIC BY BRUCE ROBISON

Two days past eighteen / He was waiting for the bus in his army greens / Sat down in a booth in a café there / Gave his order to a girl with a bow in her hair / He's a little shy so she gives him a smile / And he said would you mind sittin' down for a while / And talking to me, I'm feeling a little low / She said I'm off in an hour and I know where we can go / So they went down and they sat on the pier / He said I bet you got a boyfriend but I don't care / I got no one to send a letter to / Would you mind if I sent one back here to you / Chorus: I cried / Never gonna hold the hand of another guy / Too young for him they told her / Waitin' for the love of a travelin' soldier / Our love will never end / Waitin' for the soldier to come back again / Never more to be alone when the letter said / A soldier's coming home / So the letters came from an army camp / In California then Vietnam / And he told her of his heart / It might be love and all of the things he was so scared of / He said when it's getting kinda rough over here / I think of that day sittin' down at the pier / And I close my eyes and see your pretty smile / Don't worry but I won't be able to write for awhile / Chorus: I cried / Never gonna hold the hand of another guy / Too young for him they told her / Waitin' for the love of a travelin' soldier / Our love will never end / Waitin' for the soldier to come back again / Never more to be alone when the letter said / A soldier's coming home / One Friday night at a football game / The Lord's prayer said and the Anthem sang / A man said folks would you bow your heads / For a list of local Vietnam dead / Crying all alone under the stands / Was a piccolo player in the marching band / And one name read and nobody really cared / But a pretty little girl with a bow in her hair / Chorus: I cried / Never gonna hold the hand of another guy / Too young for him they told her / Waitin' for the love of a travelin' soldier / Our love will never end / Waitin' for the soldier to come back again / Never more to be alone when the letter says / A soldier's coming / Chorus: I cried / Never gonna hold the hand of another guy / Too young for him they told her / Waitin' for the love of the travelin' soldier / Our love will never end / Waitin' for the soldier to come back again / Never more to be alone when the letter says / A soldier's coming home

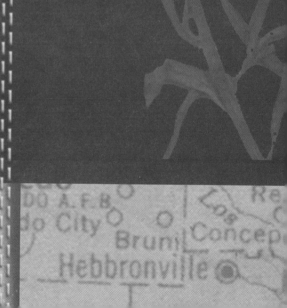

TRUTH NO. 2

WORDS & MUSIC BY PATTY GRIFFIN

You don't like the sound of the truth / Coming from my mouth / You say that I lack the proof / Well baby that might be so / I might get to the end of my life / Find out everyone was lying / I don't think that I'm afraid anymore say that I would rather die trying / Chorus: Woh-oh / Swing me way down south / Sing me something brave from your mouth / And I'll bring you / Pearls of water on my hips / And the love in my lips / All the love from my lips / This time when he swung the bat / And I found myself laying flat I wondered / What a way to spend a dime / What a way to use the time, ain't it baby / I looked at my reflection in the window walking past / And I saw a stranger / Just so scared all the time it makes me one more reason / Why the world's dangerous / Chorus: Woh-oh / Swing me way down south / Sing me something brave from your mouth / And I'll bring you / Pearls of water on my hips / And the love in my lips / All the love from my lips / You don't like the sound of the truth / Coming from my mouth / You say that I lack the proof / Well baby that might be so / Tell me what's wrong with having a little faith / In what you're feeling in your heart / Why must we be so afraid / And always so far apart / Chorus: Woh-oh / Swing me way down south / Sing me something brave from your mouth / And I'll bring you / Pearls of water on my hips / And the love in my lips / All the love from my lips

WHITE TRASH WEDDING

WORDS & MUSIC BY EMILY ROBISON, MARTIE MAGUIRE, NATALIE MAINES

You can't afford no ring / You can't afford no ring / I shouldn't be wearing white and you can't afford no ring / You finally took my hand / You finally took my hand / It took a nip of gin / But you finally took my hand / You can't afford no ring / You can't afford no ring / I shouldn't be wearing white and you can't afford no ring / Mama don't approve / Mama don't approve / Daddy says he's the best in town / And mama don't approve / You can't afford no ring / You can't afford no ring / I shouldn't be wearing white and you can't afford no ring / Baby's on its way / Baby's on its way / Say I do and kiss me quick / 'Cause baby's on its way / I shouldn't be wearing white and you can't afford no ring

A HOME

WORDS & MUSIC BY MAIA SHARP, RANDY SHARP

I mistook the warnings for wisdom / From so called friends quick to advise / Though your touch was telling me otherwise / Somehow I saw you as a weakness / I thought I had to be strong / Oh but I was just young, I was scared, I was wrong / Chorus: Not a night goes by / I don't dream of wandering / Through the home that might have been / And I listened to my pride / When my heart cried out for you / Now every day I wake again / In a house that might have been / A home / Guess I did what I did believing / That love is a dangerous thing / Oh but that couldn't hurt anymore than never knowing / Chorus: Not a night goes by / I don't dream of wandering / Through the home that might have been / And I listened to my pride / When my heart cried out for you / Now every day I wake again / In a house that might have been / A home / A home / Four walls, a roof, a door, some windows / Just a place to run when my working day is through / They say home is where the heart is / If the exception proves the rule I guess that's true / Chorus: Not a night goes by / I don't dream of wandering / Through the home that might have been / And I listened to my pride / When my heart cried out for you / Now every day I wake again / In a house that might have been / A home / A home

More Love

WORDS & MUSIC BY TIM O'BRIEN, GARY NICHOLSON

I'm so close to you baby / But I'm so far away / There's a silence between us / And there's so much to say / You're my strength, you're my weakness / You're my faith, you're my doubt / We gotta meet in the middle / To work this thing out / Chorus: More love, I can hear our hearts cryin' / More love, I know that's all we need / More love, to flow in between us / To take us and hold us and lift us above / If there's ever an answer / It's more love / We're afraid to be idle / So we fill up the days / We run on the treadmill / Keep slavin' away 'til there's no time for talkin' / About trouble in mind / And the doors are all closed / Between your heart and mine / Chorus: More love, I can hear our hearts cryin' / More love, I know that's all we need / More love, to flow in between us / To take us and hold us and lift us above / If there's ever an answer / It's more love / Just look out around us / People fightin' their wars / They think they'll be happy / When they've settled their scores / Let's lay down our weapons / That hold us apart / Be still for just a minute / Try to open our hearts / Chorus: More love, I can hear our hearts cryin' / More love, I know that's all we need / More love, to flow in between us / To take us and hold us and lift us above / If there's ever an answer / It's more love / I can hear our hearts crying / More love, I know that's all we need / More love, to flow in between us / To take us and hold us and lift us above / If there's ever an answer / It's more love / More love

I BELIEVE IN LOVE

WORDS & MUSIC BY MARTIE MAGUIRE,
NATALIE MAINES, MARTY STUART

I made a promise to myself / Locked it away deep down inside / Told my heart we'd wait it out / Swore we'd never compromise / Oh I'd rather be alone / Like I am tonight / Than settle for the kind of love / That fades before the morning light / Silence stared me in the face / And I finally heard its voice / It seemed to softly say / That in love you have a choice / Today I got the answer / And there's a world of truth behind it / Love is out there waiting somewhere / You just have to go and find it / Chorus: I believe in love / I believe in love / A love that's real, love that's strong / Love that lives on and on / Yes I believe in love / Chorus: I believe in love / I believe in love / A love that's real, love that's strong / Love that lives on and on / Yes I believe in love / Yes I believe in love

Tortured, Tangled Hearts

WORDS & MUSIC BY NATALIE MAINES,
MARTIE MAGUIRE, MARTY STUART

Well there was a little falter at the altar of confession / Down on its knees true love did fall / After 31 days of sleepless nights, she woke up to end it all / With "I love you" on a fresh tattoo engraved upon his chest / She tore her name right off his heart / So here's to the unblessed / Chorus: Oh love, oh love you fickle thing / Such pretty words and golden rings / It was a broken dream right from the start / Bless their tortured, tangled hearts / Well a blast of confusion coupled with delusion / Makes the best made plans sometimes fail / They wined and they dined, had peace of mind / She bought a gown and he rented tails / But the mighty cloud of destiny came driftin' through the gates / And busted up what could have been a perfect, hopeless case / Chorus: Oh love, oh love you fickle thing / Such pretty words and golden rings / It was a broken dream right from the start / Bless their tortured, tangled hearts / Chorus: Oh love, oh love you fickle thing / Such pretty words and golden rings / It was a broken dream right from the start / Bless their tortured, tangled hearts

LIL' JACK SLADE

MUSIC BY EMILY ROBISON, MARTIE MAGUIRE, LLOYD MAINES, TERRI HENDRIX

MARTIE: FIDDLE ✝ EMILY: BANJO ✝ LLOYD MAINES: RHYTHM GUITAR ✝ BRYAN SUTTON: GUITAR ✝ ADAM STEFFEY: MANDOLIN ✝ GLENN FUKUNAGA: BASS ✝ CHRIS THILE: MANDOLIN SOLO. PUBLISHED BY WOOLLY PUDDIN' MUSIC (BMI)/ARTMOB MUSIC/THM MUSIC (BMI) ADMINISTERED BY BUG MUSIC.

GODSPEED (SWEET DREAMS)

WORDS & MUSIC BY RADNEY FOSTER

Dragon tales and the "water is wide" / Pirate's sail and lost boys fly / Fish bite moonbeams every night / And I love you / Chorus: Godspeed, little man / Sweet dreams, little man / Oh my love will fly to you each night on angels wings / Godspeed / Sweet dreams / The rocket racer's all tuckered out / Superman's in pajamas on the couch / Goodnight moon, we'll find the mouse / And I love you / Chorus: Godspeed, little man / Sweet dreams, little man / Oh my love will fly to you each night on angels wings / Godspeed / Sweet dreams / God bless mommy and match box cars / God bless dad and thanks for the stars / God hears "Amen," wherever we are / And I love you / Chorus: Godspeed, little man / Sweet dreams, little man / Oh my love will fly to you each night on angels wings / Godspeed / Godspeed / Godspeed / Sweet dreams

Top of the World

WORDS & MUSIC BY PATTY GRIFFIN

I wished I was smarter / I wished I was stronger / I wished I loved Jesus / The way my wife does / I wish it had been easier / Instead of any longer / I wished I could have stood where you would have been proud / But that won't happen now / That won't happen now / Chorus: There's a whole lot of singing that's never gonna be heard / Disappearing everyday without so much as a word somehow / Think I broke the wings off that little song bird / She's never gonna fly to the top of the world right now / Top of the world / I don't have to answer any of these questions / Don't have no God to teach me no lessons / I come home in the evening / Sit in my chair / One night they called me for supper / But I never got up / I stayed right there in my chair / Chorus: There's a whole lot of singing that's never gonna be heard / Disappearing everyday without so much as a word somehow / Think I broke the wings off that little song bird / She's never gonna fly to the top of the world right now / I wished I'd a known you / Wished I'd a shown you / All of the things I was on the inside / I'd pretend to be sleeping / When you come in in the morning / To whisper good-bye / Go to work in the rain / I don't know why / Don't know why / 'Cause everyone's singing / We just wanna be heard / Disappearing everyday without so much as a word somehow / Wanna grab a hold of that little song bird / Take her for a ride to the top of the world right now / To the top of the world / To the top of the world / To the top of the world / To the top of the world / To the top of the world / To the top of the world / To the top of the world / To the top of the world / To the top of the world

LONG TIME GONE

Words and Music by
DARREL SCOTT

2.(Inst. solo ad lib....

...end solo) Now, me,___

Bridge:

___ I went to Nash-ville, try'n' to be the big deal. Play-in' down on Broad-way, get-tin' there the hard__ way.

Liv-in' from a tip jar, sleep-in' in my car. Hock-in' my gui-tar, yeah, I'm gon-na be__ a star.__

Verse 2:
Delia plays that ol' church piano,
Sittin' out on her daddy's farm.
She always thought that we'd be together.
Lord, I never meant to do her harm.
Said she could hear me singin' in the church choir.
Me, I heard another song.
I caught the wind and hit the road runnin'.
(To Chorus:)

Verse 3:
Now, me and Delia singin' every Sunday,
Watchin' the children and the garden grow.
We listen to the radio to hear what's cookin',
But the music ain't got no soul.
Now they sound tired but they don't sound Haggard.
They got money but they don't have Cash.
They got Junior but they don't have Hank.
I think, I think, I think the rest is...
(To Chorus:)

LANDSLIDE

Words and Music by
STEVIE NICKS

Chorus:

been a - fraid of chang - in' 'cause I built my life a - round you. But time makes you bold - er, chil - dren get old - er, I'm get - ting old - er too. Well

TRAVELIN' SOLDIER

Words and Music by
BRUCE ROBINSON

Moderately ♩ = 74

Verse:

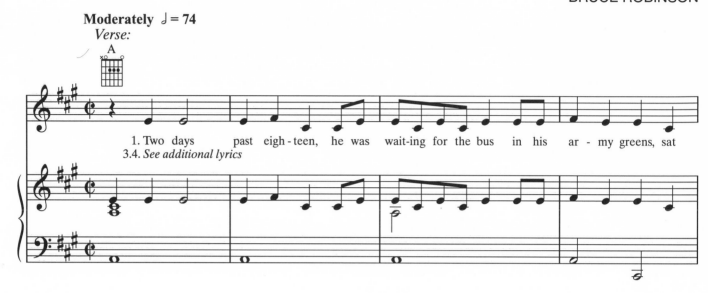

1. Two days past eigh-teen, he was wait-ing for the bus in his ar-my greens, sat
3.4. *See additional lyrics*

down in a booth in a ca-fé there,_ gave his or-der to a girl_ with a bow in her hair._

He's a lit-tle shy, so she gives him a smile, and he said would you mind sit-tin'
2. *See additional lyrics*

Travelin' Soldier - 4 - 1
PFM0221

3. So the sol-dier's com-in'. sol-dier's com-in'
4. One

home.

A

A

Repeat ad lib. and fade

D   A   D

Verse 2:
So, they went down and they sat on the pier.
He said, I bet you got a boyfriend, but I don't care.
I got no one to send a letter to,
Would you mind if I sent one back here to you?
(To Chorus:)

Verse 3:
So the letters came from an army camp,
In California, then Vietnam.
And he told her of his heart:
It might be love and all the things he was scared of.
He said when it's getting kinda rough over here,
I think of that day, sittin' down at the pier.
And I close my eyes and see your pretty smile.
Don't worry, but I won't be able to write for a while.
(To Chorus:)

Verse 4:
One Friday night at a football game,
The Lord's prayer said and the Anthem sang,
A man said, folks would you bow your head
For a list of the local Vietnam dead.
Crying all alone underneath the stands
Was a piccolo player in the marching band.
And one name read and nobody cared
But a pretty little girl with a bow in her hair.
(To Chorus:)

TRUTH NO. 2

Words and Music by
PATTY GRIFFIN

Moderate two-beat ♩ = 88

Verse:

1. You don't like the sound__ of the truth_____ com - in' from__ my mouth.__
2. 3. *See additional lyrics*

Verse 2:
This time when he swung the bat
And I found myself layin' flat, I wondered:
What a way to spend a dime,
What a way to use the time, ain't it, baby?
I looked at my reflection
In the window walkin' past, and I saw a stranger.
Just so scared all the time,
It makes me one more reason why the world's dangerous.
(To Chorus:)

Verse 3:
You don't like the sound of the truth
Comin' from my mouth.
You say that I lack the proof;
Well, baby, that might be so.
Tell me, what's wrong with havin' a little faith
In what you're feelin' in your heart?
Why must we be so afraid
And always so far apart?
(To Chorus:)

WHITE TRASH WEDDING

Words and Music by
EMILY ROBISON,
MARTIE MAGUIRE and NATALIE MAINES

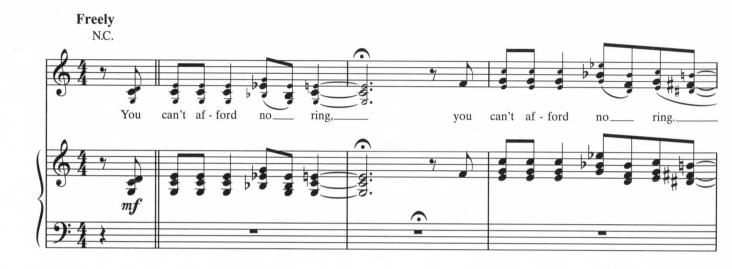

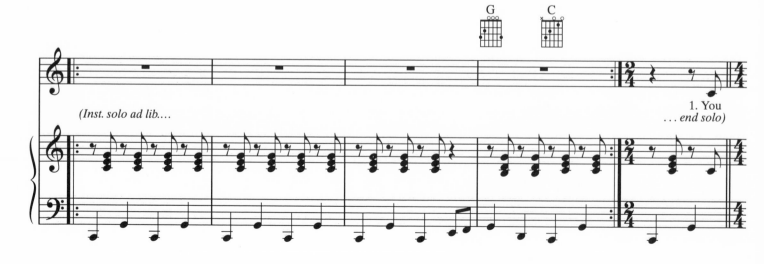

White Trash Wedding - 4 - 1
PFM0221

A HOME

Words and Music by
MAIA SHARP and RANDY SHARP

46

might___have been_____ a___ home,_____

a___ home._____

rit.

Verse 3:
Guess I did what I did believing
That love is a dangerous thing.
Oh, but that couldn't hurt anymore
Than never knowing.
(To Chorus:)

MORE LOVE

Words and Music by
TIM O'BRIEN and GARY NICHOLSON

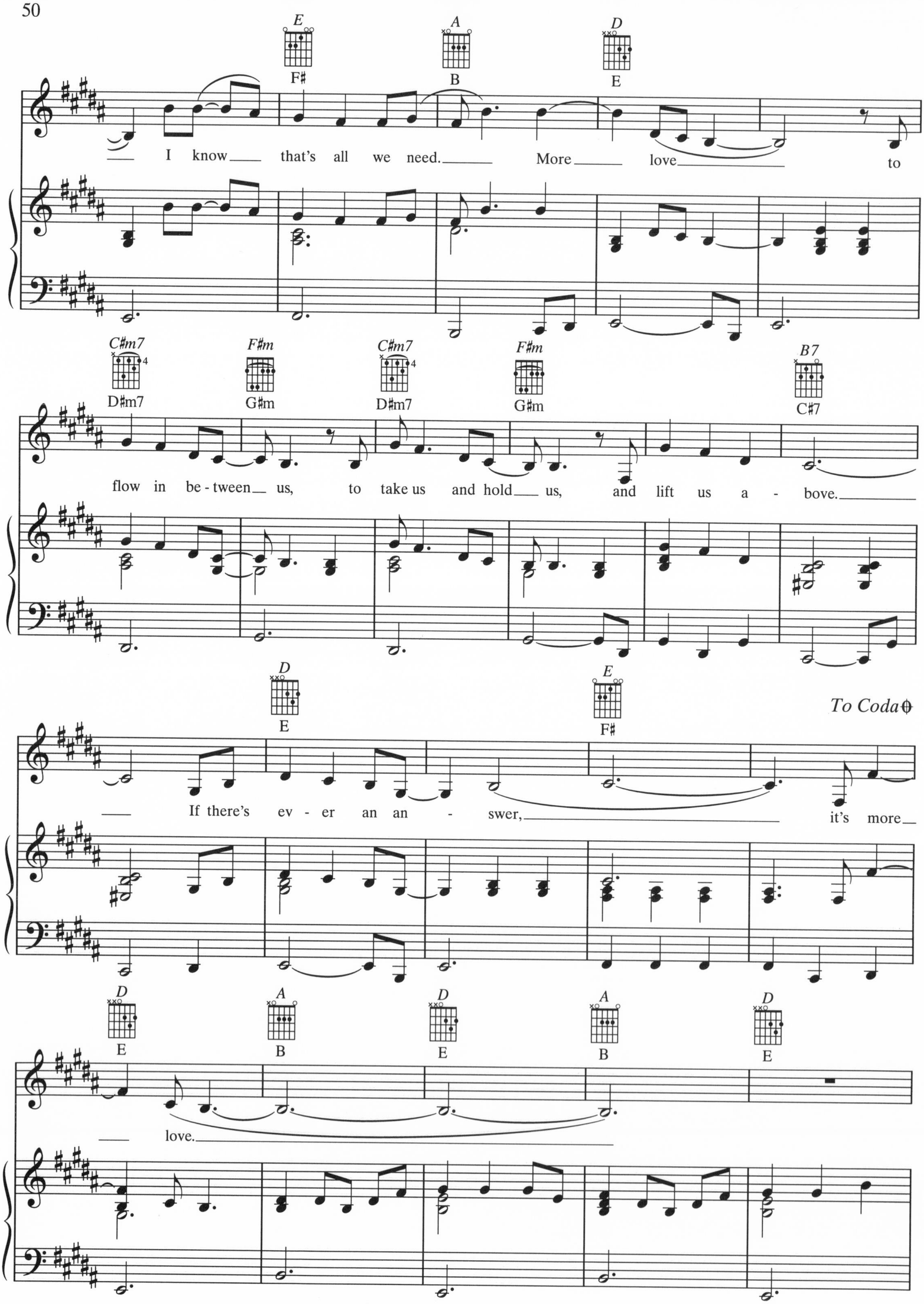

I know___ that's all we need.___ More___ love___ to

flow in be - tween___ us, to take us and hold___ us, and lift us a - bove.___

To Coda

If there's ev - er an an - swer,_____ it's more___

___ love._____

2. We're a -

Bridge:

52

Verse 2:
We're afraid to be idle, so we fill up the days,
We run on the treadmill, keep slavin' away
'Til there's no time for talkin' about trouble in mind
And the doors are all closed between your heart and mine.
(To Chorus:)

Verse 3:
Just look out around us, people fightin' their wars.
They think they'll be happy when they've settled their scores.
Let's lay down our weapons that hold us apart,
Be still for just a minute, try to open our hearts.
(To Chorus:)

I BELIEVE IN LOVE

Words and Music by
MARTIE MAGUIRE,
NATALIE MAINES and MARTY STUART

Moderately slow ballad ♩ = 80   *Verse 1:*

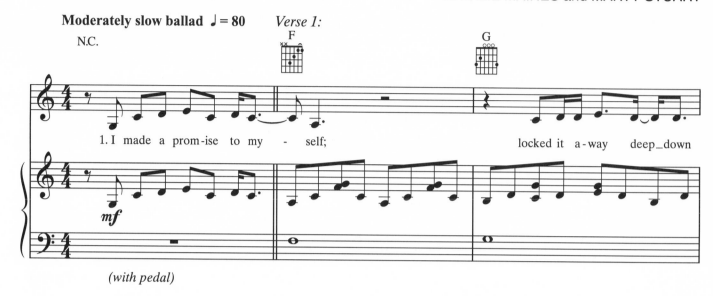

1. I made a prom-ise to my - self;   locked it a-way deep down

(with pedal)

in - side.___   Told my heart we'd__ wait it out;___

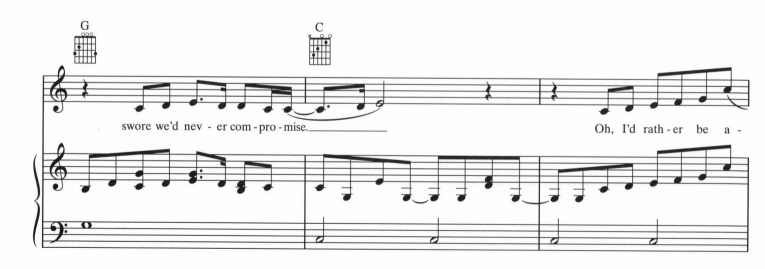

swore we'd nev - er com - pro - mise._____   Oh, I'd rath - er be a-

TORTURED, TANGLED HEARTS

Words and Music by
NATALIE MAINES,
MARTIE MAGUIRE and MARTY STUART

Bright country beat ♩ = 120

1. Well, there

Verse:

was a lit - tle fal - ter at the al - ter of con - fess - ion.
blast of__ con - fu - sion, cou - pled with__ de - lu - sion makes the

Tortured, Tangled Hearts - 9 - 1
PFM0221

60

Down on its knees,_____ true love did fall._____ Af - ter
best made_ plans_ some - time fail. They

thir - ty - one days_____ and sleep - less nights,
wine and_ one they dined,_____ had peace_____ of mind.

she woke up_____ to end_____ it all._____ With
She bought a gown and he_____ rent - ed tails. But the

"I love you,"_____ on a fresh tat - too_____ en -
might - y cloud_____ of des - tin - y_____ came

Tortured, Tangled Hearts - 9 - 5
PFM0221

LIL' JACK SLADE

Music by
EMILY ROBISON, MARTIE MAGUIRE,
LLOYD MAINES and TERRI HENDRIX

GODSPEED
(Sweet Dreams)

Words and Music by
RADNEY FOSTER

Verse:

1. Drag-on tales,___ and the "wa-ter is wide;"___ pi-rate's sail and lost___ boys fly.___
2. 3. *See additional lyrics*

(*L.H. cue notes only 1st time*)

Fish bite moon-beams ev - 'ry night,___ and I love you.____ God -

Verse 2:
The rocket racer's all tuckered out.
Superman's in pajamas on the couch.
Goodnight moon, we'll find the mouse,
And I love you.
(To Chorus:)

Verse 3:
God bless mommy and matchbox cars.
God bless dad, and thanks for the stars.
God hears "Amen" wherever we are,
And I love you.
(To Chorus:)

TOP OF THE WORLD

Words and Music by
PATTY GRIFFIN

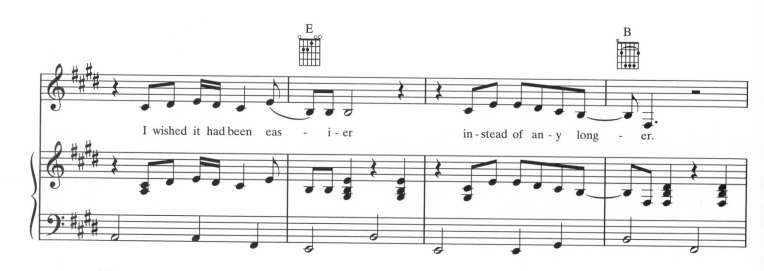

nev-er gon-na fly to the top of the world__ right now._____ Top of the

world. 2. I don't have to ___ 3. I wish I'd have known

Verse 2:
I don't have to answer any of these questions.
Don't have no God to teach me no lessons.
I come home in the evening, sit in my chair.
One night, they called me for supper, but I never got up.
I stayed right there in my chair.
(To Chorus:)

Verse 3:
I wished I'd have known you,
Wished I'd have shown you
All of the things I was on the inside.
I'd pretend to be sleeping
When you come in in the morning
To whisper goodbye, go to work in the rain.
I don't know why, don't know why.

Chorus 2:
'Cause everyone's singing, we just wanna be heard.
Disappearing everyday without so much as a word somehow.
Wanna grab a hold of that little songbird,
Take her for a ride to the top of the world right now.

THANKS ♡